W9-BRJ-099

LIGHTNING BOLT BOOKS™

Let's Look at
Sharks

Kristin L. Nelson

Lerner Publications Company

Minneapolis

Copyright © 2011 by Kristin L. Nelson

All rights reserved. International copyright secured. No part of this book may be reproduced, stored in a retrieval system, or transmitted in any form or by any means—electronic, mechanical, photocopying, recording, or otherwise—without the prior written permission of Lerner Publishing Group, Inc., except for the inclusion of brief quotations in an acknowledged review.

Lerner Publications Company
A division of Lerner Publishing Group, Inc.
241 First Avenue North
Minneapolis, MN 55401 U.S.A.

Website address: www.lernerbooks.com

Library of Congress Cataloging-in-Publication Data

Nelson, Kristin L.
     Let's look at sharks / by Kristin L. Nelson.
         p.   cm. — (Lightning bolt books™—Animal close-ups)
     Includes index.
     ISBN 978-0-7613-3894-9 (lib. bdg. : alk. paper)
     1. Sharks—Juvenile literature. I. Title.
     QL638.9.N455 2011
     597.3—dc22   2009038483

Manufactured in the United States of America
1 — BP — 7/15/10

Contents

Hunting Sharks

Sharks are good hunters. What is this shark hunting?

This shark is hunting a fish.
Chomp! The shark sinks its
teeth into the fish.

This shark eats a
fish in Hawaii.

Sharks are predators.
Predators are animals that
hunt and eat other animals.

This shark is eating a bird.
The bird is the shark's prey.
Prey is an animal that
is hunted for food.

Sharks eat many kinds of animals. Sharks eat turtles.

Sharks eat squid.

How would you find food if you were a shark?

Super Senses

A shark's sense of hearing helps it find food. A shark can hear an animal from miles away.

A shark's sense of smell helps it hunt. The holes above this shark's mouth are nostrils. Sharks smell with their nostrils.

Can you find this shark's nostrils?

Most sharks have good eyesight to help them find food. This shark can see animals that are in front of it or beside it.

Sharks also use pores to sense the movement of animals. A shark's pores are on its head.

The tiny dots on this shark's head are its pores.

Shark Teeth

Sharks have sharp teeth.

This shark has many
rows of teeth.

If it loses a tooth, a new
tooth will grow back.

Sharks have teeth on their skin too! These teeth are tiny scales called denticles.

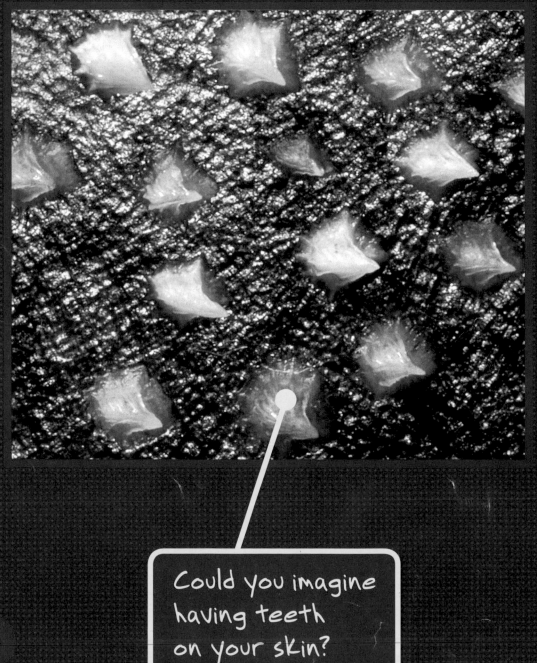

Could you imagine having teeth on your skin?

Denticles help water flow over a shark's body when it swims.

Gills and Fins

Why does this shark swim with its mouth open? A shark swims with its mouth open so it can breathe. The water goes into its mouth and flows over its gills. Gills are slits behind a shark's eyes.

These slits are the shark's gills.

Fins help sharks move and steer. The side fins are called pectoral fins. They help the shark go up or down.

These are the shark's pectoral fins.

The fins on top of a shark's body are called dorsal fins. They keep the shark from rolling over.

A shark's dorsal fin sticks out of the water.

The tail fin is called the caudal fin. It helps the shark move forward.

This female shark swims to a safe place to give birth to her babies.

Pups

Baby sharks are called pups. Most pups start as eggs that grow inside the mother.

These eggs grow safely inside a mother shark.

When it is time, the pups swim out of their mother's body. This shark is giving birth to a baby.

Some pups grow for a whole year before they are born.

Some
mother
sharks lay
their eggs on
the ocean floor.
The eggs are
protected
by egg cases.

This pup is coming out of its egg case.

Shark pups are ready to swim as soon as they are born.

Small pups can become big sharks. This shark can grow up to 12 feet (3 meters) long.

Sharks are the most powerful hunters in the ocean!

Shark Diagram

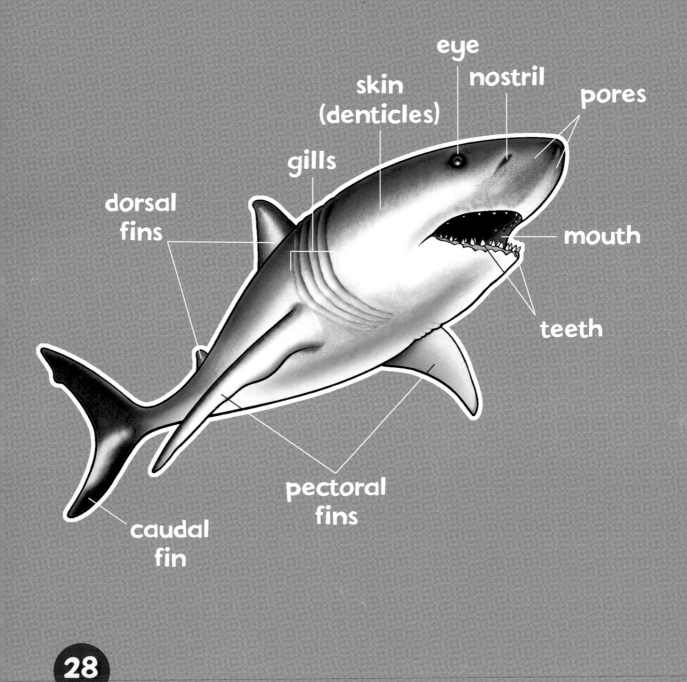

eye

nostril

pores

skin
(denticles)

gills

dorsal
fins

mouth

teeth

pectoral
fins

caudal
fin

Fun Facts

- Sharks live in waters all over the world. Most sharks live in oceans. But some live in lakes or rivers.

- The whale shark is the largest fish alive. It measures up to 60 feet (18 m) long.

- Sharks have the most powerful jaws of any creature on the planet.

- Some sharks can give birth to up to one hundred pups at a time!

- Sharks sleep with their eyes open.

Glossary

caudal fin: a shark's tail fin. The caudal fin moves from side to side to help a shark move forward.

denticle: a tiny, rough scale on a shark's skin

dorsal fin: a fin on top of a shark's body. Sharks have two dorsal fins.

egg case: a small sac that protects a mother shark's eggs on the ocean floor

gill: a slit above a shark's side fin. The shark uses its gills to breathe.

pectoral fin: a fin on a shark's side that helps it to go up or down. Sharks have two pectoral fins.

predator: an animal that hunts and eats other animals

prey: an animal that is hunted by other animals

Further Reading

Arnosky, Jim. *All about Sharks.* New York: Scholastic, 2003.

Enchanted Learning: Zoom Sharks
http://www.enchantedlearning.com/subjects/sharks

Landau, Elaine. *Scary Sharks.* Berkeley Heights, NJ: Enslow Publishers, 2003.

National Geographic Kids: Great White Sharks
http://kids.nationalgeographic.com/Animals/
CreatureFeature/Great-white-shark

Sexton, Colleen. *Sharks.* Minneapolis: Bellwether Media, 2008.

Taylor, Leighton. *Great White Sharks.* Minneapolis: Lerner Publications Company, 2006.

Index

Photo Acknowledgments

The images in this book are used with the permission of: © Richcareyzim/Dreamstime .com, p. 1; © Shawnjackson/Dreamstime.com, p. 2; © David Nardini/Getty Images, pp. 4, 30; © David Fleetham/naturepl.com, p. 5; © Zena Holloway/Getty Images, p. 6; © Tim Clark/SeaPics.com, p. 7; © Pacific Stock/SuperStock, pp. 8, 20; © Mark Conlin/ SuperStock, p. 9; © Na Gen Imaging/Getty Images, p. 10; © Stephen Frink Collection/ Alamy, pp. 11, 12; © Jeff Rotman/naturepl.com, pp. 13, 15; © Brandon Cole/Visuals Unlimited, Inc., p. 14; © Doug Perrine/Jose Castro/SeaPics.com, p. 16; © John White Photos/Getty Images, p. 17; © Papilio/Alamy, p. 18; © Melissaf84/Dreamstime.com, p. 19; © Michael Patrick O'Neill/Alamy, p. 21; © Doug Perrine/SeaPics.com, p. 22; © Doug Perrine/naturepl.com, p. 23; © Picture Partners/Alamy, p. 24; © Mark Conlin/Alamy, p. 25; © James D. Watt/SeaPics.com, p. 26; © Jean Tresfon/Getty Images, p. 27; © Laura Westlund/Independent Picture Services, p. 28; © Nejron/Dreamstime.com, p. 31.

Front cover: © Marty Snyderman/Visuals Unlimited, Inc.